INTRODUCTION

"Do good. [...] and rea[...] [...]yone

Do you ever wish the world could be a better place? Do you think that if only people could be more caring, more generous, less selfish, more loving, that the world we live in would be so different? Mahatma Gandhi, an inspirational leader in India in the early part of the 20th century, once said, "Be the change you want to see in the world." What he meant is that if we want the world to be a better place, each one of us has to change it ourselves, one action at a time. Why not start this Lent?

From Shrove Tuesday (Pancake Day) to Easter Day there is an action for you to do on six days in each week of Lent. Lent is 40 days long to match the amount of time that Jesus spent in the wilderness. Sundays are not counted because every Sunday is a reminder of Easter Day.

The actions are quite simple. What makes them challenging is how you do them and, if we all do them, then the world really could become the place that God wants it to be: one person at a time, one action at a time.

This Lent start a revolution – and be the change you want to see!

**Paula Gooder &
Peter Babington**

HOW TO USE THIS BOOK

Sometimes what we do is not as important as why we do it. *Love Life Live Lent: Be the Change* Adults' Version tries to give you the space to think about why you might be doing the LLLL actions; so the headings (Celebrate More, Say Sorry) are as important if not more so than the actions themselves. Below each heading is a quotation from the Bible followed by a brief reflection that aims to give you something to think about during the day.

Each reflection is, of course, very short and, for each subject, there is so much more that could have been said, but the point of each reflection is not to say it all but to kickstart your thinking. Inevitably some of the reflections will resonate more with you than others, but we hope that what is here will give you plenty to think about during Lent.

It is also worth noting that under each heading you could do so much more than the one action we suggest. As far as possible (except where it really doesn't work) we have tried to keep the Adults' and Children's actions the same, so that hundreds if not thousands of people will be doing the same action each day in Lent, but you aren't restricted to one action! If the reflection suggests to you that you should be doing something else ... then do that.

The things we do in Lent are not meant to be kept for Lent alone. The idea is that we learn new lessons about ourselves, about the world, and about God that we then apply for the rest of our lives. The revolution may start in Lent but can stretch outwards to change the whole of your life, maybe even the whole world – so be the change you want to see!

NOW GET STARTED!

Week 1
SHROVE TUESDAY

> "And when he comes home, he calls together his friends and neighbors, saying to them, 'Rejoice with me, for I have found my sheep that was lost.'" **Luke 15:6**

Jesus loved to celebrate and, in fact, was often criticized for feasting with the wrong kinds of people. In Luke 15, when he was criticized for feasting with sinners, Jesus told three stories, about a lost sheep, lost coin, and lost son, all of which ended with a party to celebrate the finding of something lost. The point seems to be that the Kingdom of God is exactly the place where celebration should take place, so ... celebrate more!

☐ Have a pancake party!

ASH WEDNESDAY

> "Repent, for the kingdom of heaven has come near." **Matthew 3:2**

In Matthew's Gospel, the first – and probably most important – thing that Jesus said was "Repent." This word implies changing your mind and turning and facing in a new direction. The first step on this path is to acknowledge what we have done, to say sorry to God and to anyone else we have wronged, to experience forgiveness and to turn, freed from guilt, to face the future. Jesus wants to forgive us, so ... say sorry.

☐ Think about something you have done wrong and say sorry for it.

THURSDAY
BE MORE GIVING

God is overwhelmingly generous. A wonderful story in John's Gospel, about a wedding at Cana, tells of how they ran out of wine and how Jesus made them some more – six stone jars or around 125 gallons worth. The point is that Jesus could have given them just what they needed but chose instead to be overwhelmingly generous.

Christians are called to follow Jesus and to be people of generosity, so ... be more giving.

☐ Get a jar and put your small change into it each day. At the end of Lent give it to a charity.

FRIDAY CARE FOR THOSE IN NEED

> "What does the LORD require of you but to do justice, and to love kindness, and to walk humbly with your God?" **Micah 6:8**

One of the most important words in the Old Testament is the word translated here as kindness. The problem is that this word is very hard to translate into English. It means something like faithful, loving kindness: not just a passing "niceness" but a deep down, on-going love that blossoms regularly into acts of care and thoughtfulness. As a part of our journey with him, this is what the Lord requires of us, so ... care for those in need.

☐ Watch the news. Pray for someone or something you've seen on it.

SATURDAY ENJOY OUR WORLD

> "God saw everything that he had made, and indeed, it was very good." **Genesis 1:31**

God loves the world he created. In Genesis 1, after God had done each act of creation, we are told that "it was good" and, at the end of the sixth day, when he made humanity and animals, we are told that "it was very good." However much human beings have spoiled creation since, we must not forget that God loved the world then, loves it still, and wants us to love it too, so ... enjoy our world.

☐ Plant some seeds and care for them as they grow.

SEED:

Seed Type:

Date Collected:

Collected From:

Collected By:

MONDAY

BE MORE CREATIVE

> "Thus says the LORD, your Redeemer, who formed you in the womb: I am the LORD, who made all things, who alone stretched out the heavens, who by myself spread out the earth …" **Isaiah 44:24**

God is often described in the Bible in the act of creation. Over and over again God is portrayed as stretching out the sky like a tent or patiently weaving humanity into life. God is a God of creativity, and humanity is made in his image. As we seek to be as God-like as we can, we need to try and copy God's love of bringing things to life, so … be more creative.

☐ Make something today, like a cake, a picture, a model, a poem, or a story.

TUESDAY

> "Are not two sparrows sold for a penny? Yet not one of them will fall to the ground unperceived by your Father." **Matthew 10:29**

God didn't just create the world and then walk off and leave it to itself. God continues to love and care for it.

If God cares for the world so much that God notices when one sparrow dies, just imagine

what it must feel like to see us spoiling the planet by using so much more than we need, and leaving litter behind, so ... care for the world.

☐ Turn off the lights in rooms that no one is using.

WEDNESDAY

> "But Ruth said, 'Do not press me to leave you or to turn back from following you! Where you go, I will go; where you lodge, I will lodge; your people shall be my people, and your God my God.'" **Ruth 1:16**

One of the most moving expressions of love in the whole Bible is this one from Ruth. When Naomi, her mother-in-law, tried to get her to think of herself and leave, Ruth responded with this wonderful pledge of love, loyalty, and faithfulness. We do not know whether Naomi already knew that Ruth loved her, but after it she could be in no doubt. It is much better to make sure that people know we love them because we have told them, than to assume that they know, so ... be more loving.

☐ Tell someone you love them.

THURSDAY

BE MORE CURIOUS

"When I look at your heavens, the work of your fingers, the moon and the stars that you have established; what are human beings that you are mindful of them …?" **Psalm 8:3-4**

In Psalm 8, the Psalmist looks at the world around and is moved to wonder about the place of human beings in such a complex and intricate universe. Wondering and curiosity are an essential part of human existence and have given rise to some of the most important discoveries, but so often our lives grind on with little time for us to wonder about anything, so … be more curious.

☐ Give yourself time to wonder about something and see where your curiosity leads you.

FRIDAY BE MORE GRATEFUL

> "Then one of them, when he saw that he was healed, turned back, praising God with a loud voice. He prostrated himself at Jesus' feet and thanked him." **Luke 17:15-16**

It is easy to forget to be grateful. In the story in Luke 17, ten lepers were healed, but only one of them remembered to come back and say thank you. No doubt the other nine were too busy enjoying their leprosy-free lives to remember. However, it is important to be people who are mindful of the good things.

One step towards this is to remember to say thank you more often, so ... be more grateful.

Thank you :)

☐ Say thank you to someone for who they are or what they do.

SATURDAY

NOTICE THE WORLD AROUND YOU

> "For you, O LORD, have made me glad
> by your work; at the works of your hands
> I sing for joy." **Psalm 92:4**

The world that God has made is a wonderful place: full of wonder. However, we often rush through our lives so fast that we simply do not have the time to notice quite how wonderful it is; in our busyness we miss the many different shades of green, the flowers pushing themselves through damp earth, the birds breaking into song. The world that God created really is a wonderful place, so ... notice the world around you.

☐ Walk somewhere today and notice the things around you – birds singing, sun shining, or rain splashing!

MONDAY BE MORE THANKFUL

> "O give thanks to the LORD, for he is good;
> for his steadfast love endures forever."
> **1 Chronicles 16:34**

Saying "please" and "thank you" can appear to be just about being polite but it is much more important than that. The trick lies not just in saying "thank you" but in being thankful. The more thankful we are, the more we are able to recognize the many good things that God (and others) have done for us. Saying grace before meals gives us a chance not only to say thank you but to practice being thankful too, so ... be more thankful.

☐ Say thank you to God for one of your meals today.

TUESDAY BE MORE FRIENDLY

> "You shall love your neighbor as yourself ..."
> **Leviticus 19:18**

One of the more challenging things that Jesus did in his teaching was to stretch the meaning of who our neighbors are.

The book of Leviticus had already stretched it from the people who are just like you to outsiders who live in your land; in the story of the Good Samaritan Jesus stretched it even further to include those whom we might count as our enemies.

Loving your neighbor involves far, far more than just being friendly, but it's not a bad place to start, so ...
be more friendly.

☐ Be friendly to someone new.

WEDNESDAY

"Now as you excel in everything …
so we want you to excel also in this
generous undertaking." **2 Corinthians 8:7**

What you do affects who you are. Although
popular wisdom states that bad people
do bad things and good people, good
things, it is also true that regularly acting
selfishly changes who we are just as acting
generously does. If we learn
to excel in generosity, as Paul
wanted the Corinthians to do,
then generosity stops being
just an action and becomes
instead a state of mind.
We become people whose
instinct is to rejoice in giving
things to others, so …
be more generous.

☐ Give a small
present to
someone
you know.

THURSDAY

> "The LORD God took the man and put him in the garden of Eden to till it and keep it."
> **Genesis 2:15**

In Genesis 2, one of the first things that God did after creating Adam was to make him caretaker of the Garden of Eden. Although we no longer live in that garden, the burden of care for the world that God created remains.

We are caretakers for a world we did not create and do not own. This "care-taking" extends to the whole world but begins in the places where we live, so ... make your local area cleaner.

☐ Fill a bag with litter (then put it all in the bin!).

FRIDAY

DO SOMETHING DIFFERENT

"For I do not do the good I want, but the evil I do not want is what I do." **Romans 7:19**

Evil may be putting it a bit strongly, but so often we end up by accident doing things other than the good we intended to do. It is so easy to get side-tracked, pulled into watching that bit more TV or to spend that bit more time on the computer. We don't intend to, it just happens. Sometimes all we need to do is to make the decision to do something different, some good that we meant to do but haven't, so ... do something different.

☐ Outside of work, have a screen-free day and do something different.

SATURDAY KEEP IN TOUCH MORE

> "Paul, an apostle of Christ Jesus by the will of God, and Timothy our brother, To the church of God that is in Corinth, including all the saints throughout Achaia …"
>
> **2 Corinthians 1:1**

Paul was an inveterate letter writer. Not only do we have more than ten letters from him in the New Testament, there are also allusions to many more that he wrote which didn't survive. Paul knew the importance of maintaining links with people, of hearing how they were getting on and of encouraging them for the future. If he wrote so much when communication was difficult, how much more should we communicate with those we love? So … keep in touch more.

☐ Phone someone you love but haven't seen for a while.

MONDAY

TAKE CARE OF YOUR HOME

> "Or what woman having ten silver coins, if she loses one of them, does not light a lamp, sweep the house, and search carefully until she finds it?" **Luke 15:8**

The point of the parable of the lost coin is that the woman cares so deeply for the lost coin that she will stop at nothing until it is found. Of course in its context this parable is about searching for *people* that are lost and not just *things*. So why not take this parable one step further? And while you tidy a room or cupboard, pray for someone who is lost or who has lost their way, so ... take care of your home.

☐ Tidy a room or a closet in your house.

TUESDAY BE MORE OPEN

"See, the former things have come to pass, and new things I now declare …" **Isaiah 42:9**

One of the characteristics of human beings is that we often like things to be the same as they've always been. Just think about how outraged you feel when they move the supermarket shelves around or change something you love. Although we don't like it, change is important for us, because it stops us becoming stagnant and inert. God is always doing something new, so … be more open.

☐ Try something new, for example a different food or a new experience.

WEDNESDAY

> "Greet one another with a holy kiss."
> **Romans 16:16**

Well maybe not a kiss – it would certainly surprise your neighbors if you tried to kiss them! However, the sentiment remains. So many people live in an isolated and lonely bubble, with no one to reach out to them and understand who they really are.

Neighbors can be near us physically but a long, long way away in all other senses. Being a good neighbor involves reaching out and being "near" in more ways than just living nearby, so ... be a good neighbor.

☐ Say hi to your neighbors today or when you next see them.

THURSDAY BE MORE PEACEFUL

> "And the peace of God, which surpasses all understanding, will guard your hearts and your minds in Christ Jesus." **Philippians 4:7**

Peace is not something that can be instilled by command. Indeed, it is often the case that the more that people tell you to be calm and relaxed, the more agitated and stressed you feel. The peace that Paul talks about in Philippians is not the kind you need to work to achieve: it is God's, and it will guard us. We do not need to strive after it so much as to allow it to encompass us, so … be more peaceful.

☐ Listen to a piece of music that makes you feel relaxed.

FRIDAY HAVE MORE FUN

> "You show me the path of life. In your presence there is fullness of joy; in your right hand are pleasures for evermore."
> **Psalm 16:11**

There is a widespread belief that the Christian faith is so serious and important that there can be no room for fun. In fact, Christian life and faith is so very important that the only thing to do is to enjoy it, with all the fullness of joy that is to be found in God's presence.

If we seek to express this joy in our lives, one way of doing that must surely involve having fun, so … have more fun.

☐ Do something today "just" for fun.

SATURDAY THINK OF OTHERS MORE

> "Love one another with mutual affection;
> outdo one another in showing honor."
> **Romans 12:10**

In our culture, love has become an emotion: one that you either have or don't have. In the Bible, however, it seems much more closely coupled with action; there love is not so much what you feel but what you do; there you love people by giving them honor and by putting their needs above your own.

How we feel about other people is much less important than how we treat them, so …

think of others more.

☐ Do a job that someone else normally does, like washing the dishes or taking out the trash.

MONDAY SAVE WATER

> "He gives rain on the earth and sends waters on the fields …" **Job 5:10**

There is no space here to address the complex – indeed nigh on impossible – question of why some of us have all the water we need, while others have either far too much or none at all. But one thing is certain: water, the kind that nourishes us and brings life, is a gift not a right. As a result, it is something to give constant thanks for and to preserve, not to squander, so … save water.

☐ Use the dish water to water some plants.

TUESDAY **CARE FOR YOUR FRIENDS MORE**

> "And may the Lord make you increase and abound in love for one another and for all, just as we abound in love for you."
>
> **1 Thessalonians 3:12**

Love is a vital theme in the New Testament: love both for those outside our natural circles but also for those within them. The early Christian writer, Tertullian, noted that non-Christians often said, "See how these Christians love one another." Would people notice the same thing of Christians today? Our challenge is to become people so overflowing with love that it spills outwards to all those around us, so … care for your friends more.

☐ Make a list of your friends' birthdays and remember to send them birthday cards.

WEDNESDAY

> "Bear one another's burdens, and in this way you will fulfil the law of Christ."
> **Galatians 6:2**

We live in a world of information overload. The Internet – and in particular social networking sites – allows us to have passing knowledge about the day-to-day lives of many people so that we often know a little about a lot of people but not a lot about any of them. Bearing one another's burdens involves not just knowing a few details but knowing so much about their griefs and joys that we carry them in our hearts, so … listen more carefully.

☐ Ask someone how they are and take time to listen to the answer.

THURSDAY SLOW DOWN

"O taste and see that the LORD is good ..."
Psalm 34:8

We live in a world that whirls by at ever increasing speeds. Not only do we travel quickly, we do everything else quickly too. There is nothing inherently wrong with this, but it can mean that we go at such a speed that we forget to savor the good things that we have. The ability to savor is a frame of mind, and if we become better at tasting our cornflakes, we might discover that we get better at savoring other good things too, so ... slow down.

☐ Take longer over breakfast and really taste your cornflakes (or whatever else you have!).

FRIDAY

THINK MORE POSITIVELY

> "I will tell of all your wonderful deeds."
> **Psalm 9:1**

Are you a glass half full or a glass half empty person? We are used to associating positivity with personality types, and there is no doubt that there are some people who are naturally more optimistic than others, but thinking positively can also be a discipline. We can see the bad everywhere we look, or we can train ourselves to look for the good. As Christians we are called to be tellers of good news, so … think more positively.

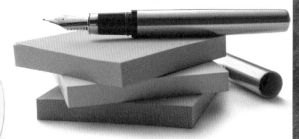

☐ Make a list of all the good things in your life and thank God for them.

SATURDAY

> "Now the whole group of those who believed were of one heart and soul, and no one claimed private ownership of any possessions, but everything they owned was held in common." **Acts 4:32**

The earliest Christians shared everything that they had, though even in the earliest days they struggled with it (look at chapter 5 of Acts for signs of it going wrong). Over the years Christians have tried (and often failed) to return to the principle of sharing everything that they own, but this failure doesn't mean we should give up on sharing. If sharing everything is unrealistic, sharing as much as we can is something we can all aim for, so … share more.

☐ Make some cupcakes and share them with your friends.

MONDAY **BE STILL**

> "Be still, and know that I am God!"
> **Psalm 46:10**

How often do you take the time to be deeply and profoundly still? If you are inexperienced at it, it can be incredibly difficult: your body may twitch or your mind wander off.

Hard as it is, it is worth doing not least because then, when all other distractions are gone, we can discover more about who we are and how we really feel about things, but also, more importantly, we open up a space in which we can encounter God, so … be still.

☐ Sit still for five minutes and listen to your breathing.

TUESDAY BE MORE WELCOMING

> "Do not neglect to show hospitality to strangers, for by doing that some have entertained angels without knowing it."
> **Hebrews 13:2**

The gift of hospitality is something we are often not very good at. Anyone who has experienced the open, generous welcome that strangers often receive in other countries will know quite how bad we are at hospitality. But hospitality – the ability to reach beyond ourselves and welcome those we don't know – is a gift that transforms not only the one who is welcomed but also the one who offers welcome, so …
be more welcoming.

☐ Invite someone you don't know very well to come for tea.

WEDNESDAY

> "Finally, beloved, whatever is true, whatever is honorable, whatever is just, whatever is pure, whatever is pleasing, whatever is commendable, if there is any excellence and if there is anything worthy of praise, think about these things." **Philippians 4:8**

What do you spend most of your time thinking about? For each of us the answer will be different. In Philippians, Paul urges his readers to make sure they spend most time thinking about good things – things that are honorable and worthy of praise – not the many other things that can so easily crowd our minds. This thinking about honorable things is a discipline that can take many forms, but one of them is to use our imagination to think about the welfare of those around us, so … be more thoughtful.

☐ Think about what might make someone you know happy, then do it!

THURSDAY

SMILE MORE

> "O that we might see some good! Let the light of your face shine on us, O LORD!"
> **Psalm 4:6**

Somewhat intriguingly, in the Old Testament, a phrase that is commonly used to describe the good things we receive from God refers to the light of God's face, as here, or in the well-loved blessing from Numbers 6:25, "The LORD make his face to shine upon you." The phrase ties up blessing with smiling. While smiling is no substitute for doing good in the world, smiling communicates things such as warmth, love and joy, which are all part of God's blessing to us, so … smile more.

☐ Give lots of smiles away today.

FRIDAY BE AWARE OF OTHERS

> "My brothers and sisters, do you with your acts of favoritism really believe in our glorious Lord Jesus Christ?" **James 2:1**

It's all too easy to show favoritism. Jesus recognized our tendency to be nice only to our friends and family (see Luke 14:12), and James saw that the rich and famous so often get preferential treatment. Following Jesus means trying to avoid showing favoritism to those we might feel more comfortable with and going out of our way to love and care for those who would not normally catch our attention, those who might slip under our radar and remain unnoticed, so … be aware of others.

☐ Make a list of up to five people you have met today, and then pray for them.

SATURDAY

> "Take no gold, or silver, or copper in your belts, no bag for your journey, or two tunics, or sandals, or a staff; for laborers deserve their food." **Matthew 10:9-10**

When Jesus first sent his disciples out to proclaim the kingdom, he told them to take nothing extra with them other than the clothes they stood up in. The call to simple living is not an easy one to follow – sometimes it can feel as if our possessions increase all on their own – but the call is still important. Simplicity of living offers fewer distractions and the potential for greater focus on the things that are important, so … live more simply.

☐ Find something you don't use and give it away.

"And we urge you, beloved, to admonish the idlers, encourage the faint-hearted, help the weak, be patient with all of them."
1 Thessalonians 5:14

Although the childhood rhyme declares that "sticks and stones can

WELL DONE

break my bones but words can never hurt me," we all know that it isn't really true. Unkind words stick like barbs to our souls and rise up to haunt us at the most unexpected times. On the other hand, genuine encouragement – the recognition that something we have done is good or has made a difference – is a balm to the soul and vital for well-being, so ... be more encouraging.

GREAT

☐ Find ways to encourage those around you today.

TUESDAY

"[Jesus] said, … 'Do this in remembrance of me.'" **1 Corinthians 11:24**

Christians believe that Jesus is present with us when we remember him as he told us to. This is a little like when we say that we know something "by heart"; it is more than just a memory in our brains, it somehow lives deep within us. Special words known by heart can inspire, nourish, and sustain us when we need them most as we recite them or bring them to mind, so … remember more.

☐ Learn the words of something by heart, for example a poem, a prayer, or a song.

WEDNESDAY

> "The wicked borrow, and do not pay back, but the righteous are generous and keep giving …" **Psalm 37:21**

Giving someone a present once can be quite easy, the second time can be quite straightforward too, but what happens if, like the righteous of Psalm 37, you are generous and keep on giving? How then do you know what to give? The answer lies in love and in imagination. It is too easy when you love someone to fall back into worn grooves of giving – like socks or flowers – but real love which yearns for the very best for our loved ones digs deep into imagination and gives them something really precious, so … be more imaginative.

☐ Find out what someone has given up for Lent – and buy it for them as an Easter present.

THURSDAY LOVE ONE ANOTHER

"I give you a new commandment, that you love one another. Just as I have loved you, you also should love one another." **John 13:34**

People often talk a lot about the Ten Commandments. They are, of course, important, but even more important for Christians is the one commandment of Jesus. Jesus taught his disciples a lot, he told many stories, he lived a life that we can follow, but he only gave one explicit commandment: love one another. It is very straightforward but profoundly difficult to do. Hard as it is, it is the only direct commandment that Jesus gave, so ... love one another.

☐ If the seeds you planted have grown enough, give some away. If not, buy a plant or some flowers for someone.

FRIDAY

> "Then Jesus said, 'Father, forgive them; for they do not know what they are doing.'"
> **Luke 23:34**

At the heart of God is love, and at the heart of that love is forgiveness. That loving forgiveness is revealed definitively in Jesus' death on the cross. It cannot be fully explained, adequately expressed, or completely understood. All we can do is use our hearts, minds, and imaginations to enter into the story, so ... today find time to think about the Good Friday story.

☐ Make an Easter Garden or read Luke 22–24 (or both!).

SATURDAY

> "Mary Magdalene went and announced to the disciples, 'I have seen the Lord'…"
> **John 20:18**

Think of the last time you had something exciting to tell a friend. Whether it was about a birth, a job opportunity, or a great bargain at the mall, it's not hard to share good news. One of the striking features of many of the resurrection accounts is that those who have seen the risen Christ simply cannot contain their excitement: they rush back from their encounter to share the good news with their friends. The new life, fresh hope, and sheer joy of Easter is the best news ever, so … share the Easter story.

☐ Give someone an Easter Card (even better make it first!).